# Diet recommendations for TCM - Large intestine - external cold affects the colon

Please check these recommendations always with a TCM nutrition consultant, therapist, doctor or dietician. The recipes and the list of ingredients are supporting also the conventional medical therapy. The calorie disclosures of fresh ingredients (fruit and vegetables) vary according to quality and time of harvest. The contents were checked by a dietician and a nutrition consultant for the Traditional Chinese Medicine (TCM).

Author:
©2017 Josef Miligui
www.ebns.at

AF285340

Source:
The lists are created from the EBNS database for nutritional counseling. The database is used by dietitians, therapists and doctors for advising the patient / client.

Literature:
The specialist literature and the training documents of the German and Austrian dietary and traditional Chinese medicine serve as a knowledge base. We have used the documents as a basis of knowledge, adapted it to our experience and completed them.
http://di-book.com

Title Photo:
©2008 Erika Weixlbaumer

Production and publishing:
BoD – Books on Demand, Norderstedt
ISBN: 9783752861211

# Diet recommendations for TCM - Large intestine - external cold affects the colon

# 1 Treatment strategy

Expel cold, move qi, warm.

# 2 Avoid

-

# 3 Breakfast

|  | kkal. per serving |
| --- | --- |
| Beef soup with colorful vegetables and mushrooms | 142 |
| Chickpeas with Raisins | 429 |
| Coconut rice with cardamom | 266 |
| Hummus (Chickpeasmash) | 542 |
| Leek soup with almondmash | 115 |
| Legumes | 31 |
| Millet with egg and butter | 338 |
| Pea dish | 406 |
| Plums with curd cheese | 141 |
| Polenta with fried egg | 410 |
| Polenta with ratatouille | 225 |
| Quick flakes with compote or jam | 189 |
| Quinoa piquant with avocado | 561 |
| Quinoa with peach | 247 |
| Radish with horseradish | 196 |
| Reissue soup with fresh fruits | 143 |
| Rice congee with crushed walnuts | 406 |
| Rice congee with dried fruit | 210 |
| Rice dulse soup | 190 |
| Rice noodle soup with shiitake mushrooms | 65 |

## 4   Snack

## 5   Lunch

# 6   Afternoon

# 7   Dinner

# 8   Any time

# 9 Recipes

(recommendable) = You can use more.
(little) = You should use less than specified or omit.

## 9.1 8 treasures of rice

Strengthens kidney and bladder, builds up Qi, strengthens the spleen, repels moisture, reduces internal heat, prevents cancer, builds heart, calms nerves.
Cooking time approx. 1 hour
Calories p. portion: 212
4 portions

### Quantity of ingredients
Lily bulbs  1 table spoon / 5g. ........................................................ *
Longane  1 table spoon / 5g. ........................................................ *
King Solomon's-seal  1 table spoon / 5g. ....................................... *
Yam root, yam root tuber  1 table spoon / 5g. ................................ *
Coix (seeds) YiYi Ren  1 table spoon / 5g. ..................................... *
Rice wild (nature rice)  1 1/2 cups / 240g. .................................. metal
Water  8-10 cups / 800g. (yes) .................................................. earth

### Cooking instructions:
Each one 1 tbsp:  Bai He, Longan, Yu Zhu, Da Zao, Shan Yao, Lian Mi, Yi Yi Ren, Qian Shi
Add hot water and soak for about 30 minutes. Then add 1 - 2 cups of rice (normal) and simmer for 1/2 to 1 hour until the rice is very soft. Or: Cook for about 3 hours with the herbs a congee. Then the herbs do not have to be soaked.

## 9.2 Basic recipe for a beef broth (clear)

Strengthens Qi and Yang, is very warming.
Cooking time approx. 4-8 hours
Calories p. portion: 114
10 portions
Allergens: O

### Quantity of ingredients
Beef soup meat  1,1 lbs / 500g. ............................................... earth
Beef meatbones  5/8 oz / 200g. ............................................... earth
Vinegar (Red wine vinegar)  1 dash / 3g. ................................... wood
Juniper berry  8 pieces / 6g. ...................................................... fire

Rosemary  1 pinch /  1g.  ............................................................. fire
Carrot  3 pieces /  210g.  ......................................................... earth
Parsnip  2 pieces /  300g.  ......................................................... fire
Leek  1 piece /  200g.  ...............................................................metal
Ginger fresh  1/2 teaspoon /  5g.  ...........................................metal
Lovage  1 stem /  15g.  ...............................................................metal
Clove  2 pieces /  2g.  ................................................................metal
Pimento  6 pieces /  12g.  ..........................................................metal
Anise (Common Fennel)  2 pieces /  1g.  ................................. earth
Salt  1 teaspoon /  5g.  ............................................................water
Water  3,3 lbs /  1300g.  ........................................................... earth

**Cooking instructions:**
Heat water, a dash of red wine vinegar, some juniper berries, a little
rosemary, bones and meat till it boils; add carrot, parsnip, leek, ginger,
lovage, clove, allspice, star anise and a little salt; simmer for 4-8 hours
then strain. Refrigerate for later use.

## 9.3    Basic recipe for a chicken broth worming

Strengthens Qi and blood, is very warm.
Cooking time approx. 2-3 hours
Calories p. portion: 90
9 portions
Allergens: L

**Quantity of ingredients**
Chicken meat  1/2 piece /  600g.  .............................................wood
Carrot  2 pieces /  150g.  ......................................................... earth
Leek  1 stick /  45g.  .................................................................metal
Celery root  1 piece /  500g.  ................................................... earth
Ginger fresh  2 slices /  2g. ....................................................metal
Fenugreek  (Trigonella foenum-graecum)  1 teaspoon /  2g.  .............*
Juniper berry  1 teaspoon /  3g.  ................................................ fire
Bay leaf  3 pieces /  2g.  ................................................................*
Water  4 cup /  900g.  ............................................................... earth

**Cooking instructions:**
Remove chicken parts from fat. Place chicken pieces in a saucepan with
hot water and heat till it boils briefly, skimming any resulting foam. Add
coarsely chopped vegetables and all spices and cook over medium heat
for 2 to 3 hours. Strain the finished soup. Throw away vegetables and
bones.

Tip: If you want to use the meat as a soup insert, take out after 45 minutes and return only the bones in the soup.
Refrigerate for later use.

## 9.4   Basic recipe for a fish broth

Strengthens kidney Qi and Yin, strengthens blood and fluids, promotes urination.
Cooking time approx. 40 min
Calories p. portion: 128
5 portions
Allergens: DLO

**Quantity of ingredients**
Fish pieces mixed (fresh water)  3/4 lbs / 300g.  .........................water
Celery root  1/4 lbs - 4oz / 120g.  ............................................. earth
Leek  2 inches / 10g.  .............................................................metal
Carrot  2 pieces / 150g.  .......................................................... earth
White wine  1/2 cup / 125g.  ..................................................... wood
Lemon  1/2 piece / 50g.  .......................................................... wood
Bay leaf  2 leaves / 2g.  ................................................................*
Peppercorns  3 pieces / 2g.  ...................................................metal
Olive oil  1 table spoon / 10g.  .................................................. earth
Water  2 cup / 450g.  ............................................................... earth

**Cooking instructions:**
Fry celery, chopped carrots and leeks in olive oil, add bay leaf and peppercorns, add pieces of fish and sauté briefly. Add water, add little white wine or lemon. Simmer gently for 30 minutes. Skim off the resulting foam several times. In the end, sift the ingredients through a cloth.
Refrigerate for later use.

## 9.5   Basic recipe for a reissue soup (Congee)

Warms the stomach and spleen, harmonizes the intestine, forces Qi, reduces moisture.
Cooking time approx. 2-4 hours
Calories p. portion: 140
3 portions
Allergens:

**Quantity of ingredients**
Rice variety any  1 cup / 120g.  .................................................metal
Water  6 cups / 700g.  ............................................................. earth

**Cooking instructions:**
Cook rice and water in a ratio of about 1: 6. The amount of water determines the thickness of the mash (matter of taste).
Put the rice in a saucepan with a heavy lid. It is important to simmer the rice after a short boil on the slightest flame, otherwise it burns.
Boil the rice for 2-4 hours. The longer he cooks, the more he strengthens. If you want to eat the dish for breakfast, you can put the rice on just before bedtime.
To be on the safe side, you should first check the behavior of your pot and cooker under observation for a similar amount of time, so that nothing burns.
Refrigerate for later use.

## 9.6 Beef soup with carrots, leeks, bay leaves

Strengthens spleen Qi, strengthens blood and Qi, moisturizes, relaxes, builds up Qi, spreads, strengthens spleen and liver, regulates Qi flow, strengthens stomach Qi.
Cooking time approx. 2-3 hours
Calories p. portion: 194
5 portions

**Quantity of ingredients**
Beef meat  1 lbs /  500g. .......................................................... earth
Carrot  2 pieces /  200g. ........................................................... earth
Leek  1/2 piece /  150g. ............................................................metal
Bay leaf  3 leaves /  1g. ...................................................................*
Corn Grease (Polenta)  1 table spoon /  10g. ............................. earth
Water  2 cup /  450g. (yes) ....................................................... earth
Salt  1 pinch /  0,5g. ................................................................water

**Cooking instructions:**
In a saucepan with water (enough to cover the meat), add beef soup meat or leg slice and simmer for a moment; then pour off the broth, rinse the meat with hot water (this will save you from foaming), clean the pot and put the meat in hot water again; add chopped carrot, leek, corn and bay leaf; simmer until the meat is cooked.

## 9.7 Beef soup with colorful vegetables and mushrooms

Nourishing and slightly warming, builds up Qi and fluids, strengthens spleen Qi, strengthens blood and Qi, relaxes, builds up Qi, spreads, moves Qi and blood, diuretic, nourishes lung Yin, produces humors.
Cooking time approx. 2-6 hours
Calories p. portion: 142
6 portions
Allergens: EO

**Quantity of ingredients**
Water  3 cups /  700g. (yes) ........................................................ earth
Lemon  1 dash /  2g. ................................................................. wood
Pepper powder (hot)  1 pinch /  0,3g. ................................................ fire
Beef meat  1,1 lbs /  500g. .......................................................... earth
Broccoli  1 cup cutted /  100g. ...................................................... earth
Kohlrabi  1 cup diced /  100g. ....................................................... earth
Ginger fresh  1 inch /  3g. ........................................................... metal
Oregano fresh  2 table spoons /  6g. ................................................ metal
Soy sauce  1 dash /  1g. ............................................................. water
White wine  2 table spoons /  20g. ................................................. wood
Oyster mushroom  4-6 pieces /  20g. ................................................ earth
Chinese cabbage  3-4 table spoons (cut) /  30g. ......................... earth
Pepper (ground)  1 pinch /  0,2g. .................................................. metal
Onion (spring onion)  2-3 pieces /  50g. ..................................... metal
Salt  1 pinch /  0,5g. ............................................................... water

**Cooking instructions:**
Heat in a saucepan with water (enough to cover the meat), a dash of lemon juice, a pinch of rose paprika, beef stew or leg slice, till it boils and simmer for a moment; then pour off the broth, rinse the meat with hot water (this will save you from foaming), clean the pot and put the meat in hot water again; chopped stalks of broccoli, chopped kohlrabi, a piece of sliced ginger; simmer until the meat is cooked; abundant dried oregano, Add soy sauce, white wine or lemon juice, some rose paprika or fresh oregano, oyster mushrooms cut into strips or shiitake mushrooms, add the broccoli florets, chopped Chinese cabbage; simmer until the ingredients are cooked; ground pepper, add plenty of chopped green onions; simmer briefly, season with salt, lemon juice.

## 9.8 Beluga lentil stew with vegetables

Tonifies Qi and blood, forces kidneys and spleen, dissipates heat and moisture.
Cooking time approx. 20 min
Calories p. portion: 201
5 portions

**Quantity of ingredients**
Lentils  1 1/2 cups /  240g. .......................................................water
Water  4-5 cups /  500g. (yes) .................................................. earth
Carrot  3 pieces /  150g. ........................................................... earth
Leek  1 piece /  300g. ...............................................................metal
Kohlrabi  1/2 piece /  200g. ...................................................... earth
Tomato  2 pieces /  80g. ...........................................................wood
Onion white  1 piece /  50g. .....................................................metal
Bay leaf  2 leaves /  1g. .................................................................. *
Fennel  1 piece /  250g. ............................................................ earth
Star anise  2 pieces /  1g. ............................................................... *
Juniper berry  6 pieces /  2g. ...................................................... fire
Olive oil  2 table spoons /  30g. ............................................... earth
Salt  1 pinch /  1g. ....................................................................water
Ginger fresh  1/2 teaspoon /  2g. ..............................................metal
Black caraway  1 pinch /  1g. .......................................................... *

**Cooking instructions:**
Heat oil in hot pot. Fry onions and add diced vegetables and spices, lentils (washed well) and salt. Cover with cold
 water (3 fingers wide) and cook for 20 minutes on a low heat.
Sprinkle with fresh herbs and black cumin

Goes well with rice!


## 9.9 Black-eyed beans stew

Strengthens spleen and kidney, is very nutritious, warms the stomach and spleen, harmonizes the intestine, forces Qi, strengthens stomach and kidney, strengthens spleen and kidney.
Cooking time approx. 20 min
Calories p. portion: 140
5 portions

**Quantity of ingredients**

Black-eyed peas  1 cup /  100g. ...............................................water
Rice variety any  1 1/2 cups /  200g. ........................................metal
Water  10 cups /  1000g. (yes)................................................. earth

**Cooking instructions:**
Soak the beans overnight and strain.

In a ratio of 1: 2, simmer the beans together with the rice in the Water. Depending on how hot the flame is and how
 thin the dish should be, more water must be added.

Variation: Add vegetables fried in oil, such as carrots, celery tubers, onions or leeks.

## 9.10  Boiled fillet with potatoebiscuits (Austrian classic Tafelspitz)

Strengthens spleen Qi, strengthens blood and Qi, moisturizes, relaxes, builds up Qi, spreads, forces Qi, forces spleen, relieves inflammation, moisturizes.
Cooking time approx. 3 hours
Calories p. portion: 454
8 portions
Allergens: L

**Quantity of ingredients**

Onion white  1 piece /  50g. .....................................................metal
Corn germ oil  1 table spoon /  10g. ......................................... earth
Water  32 cup - 1 gallon /  0g. (yes)........................................... earth
Beef meat  5,4 lbs - 70oz cap of rump /  1800g. .......................... earth
Beef meatbones  4n slices with bone marrow /  0g. .................... earth
Salt  1 pinch /  0,5g. ...............................................................water
Peppercorns  15 pieces /  0g. ...................................................metal
Parsnip  1 piece /  0g. ................................................................ fire
Carrot  2 pieces /  0g. .............................................................. earth
Celery root  1 slice /  0g. .......................................................... earth
Parsley root  2 pieces /  0g. ..................................................... earth
Leek  1/2 stick /  0g. ................................................................metal
Chives  1 table spoon (chopped) /  7g. .....................................metal
Potato  2,2 lbs /  1000g. ........................................................... earth
Sunflower oil  2 table spoons /  20g. ........................................ earth
Salt  1 pinch /  0,5g. ...............................................................water

**Cooking instructions:**
Halve the onions, but do not peel. Brown onions in a pan with fat on the cut surfaces very dark. Wash meat and bones briefly with warm water, drain.
Heat the water till it boils, put in meat and cook gently. Always scoop up rising foam. As soon as no more foam rises, add peppercorns and the onion. Clean and cut root and leeks and add after about two and a half hours cooking time. Simmer for another half hour.
Remove boiled beef from the soup, pour through a sieve and season with salt. Cut roots into bite-sized pieces. Add the soup together with the marrow bones and leave it under the boiling point. Cut the boiled beef into finger-
thick slices against the grain, place in the soup, heat again, sprinkle with a little chives.
In addition, cook and peel the potatoes in salted water. Stomp roughly or cut finely. Fry in a pan with the oil crispy.

## 9.11 Carp soup

Nourishing and slightly warming, strengthens the middle and the lower heater, removes moisture.
Cooking time approx. 2 hours
Calories p. portion: 499
2 portions
Allergens: DO

**Quantity of ingredients**
Carp  1,1 lbs /  500g. ...............................................................water
Salt  1 pinch /  1g. ...................................................................water
Vinegar (Apple vinegar)  1 teaspoon /  3g. ................................ wood
Thyme  1 Twig /  3g. ...........................................................................*
Juniper berry  8 pieces /  3g. ........................................................ fire
Carrot  2 pieces /  200g. ......................................................... earth
Leek  1 piece /  200g. ............................................................metal
Onion white  1 piece /  60g. .....................................................metal
Ginger fresh  1/2 teaspoon /  2g. ..............................................metal
Bay leaf  3 leaves /  1g. .....................................................................*
White wine  1/2 cup /  125g. .................................................... wood
Basil  3 leaves /  1g. ...............................................................metal

**Cooking instructions:**
Preparation: When shopping at the fishmonger, remove the fillets from a medium-sized, whole carp and also pack the fish head, spine with bones and tail.

Cut the fillets into 1 cm cubes; salt and set aside.

Place fish head, backbone and tail of carp in plenty of cold water; heat till it boils and scoop the foam; add a dash of vinegar, a fresh sprig of thyme, juniper berries; Add carrot, a piece of leek and chopped onion; add a thick slice of ginger, some peppercorns, 1 bay leaf, salt; simmer for about 1 1/2 hours and pour the stock through a sieve.

Put the carp pieces in a saucepan; pour a shot of white wine; Add rose paprika, basil leaves, finely ground carrots, dried thyme and the stock and warm; Boil the ingredients for about 5 minutes until the fish pieces are cooked.
Variants: Thicken the soup with kudzu or mashed potatoes.
This fits: baguette and dry white wine.


## 9.12 Chicken soup with angelica root and buckthorn fruit

Strengthens spleen and nourishes the blood and Yin of the liver, forces Qi and blood, is very warming.
Cooking time approx. 1 1/2 hours
Calories p. portion: 77
3 portions
Allergens: LO

**Quantity of ingredients**
Basic recipe for a chicken soup (warming)  2 cup /  500g. .................*
Angelica root  1/8 oz /  5g. ................................................................*
Bocksdorn fruits, goji berry dried  1/8 lbs - 2oz /  50g. ................ wood

**Cooking instructions:**
When you cook chicken broth according to basic recipes add angelica root and willowberry fruits in the last 40 minutes.

Ingestion: Drink 2-3 cups of broth daily.

## 9.13 Chickpeas with Raisins

Strengthens spleen and liver, regulates Qi flow, moisturizes, relaxes, builds up Qi, spreads, strengthens spleen and heart, softens, passes downwardly, warms the stomach and spleen, harmonizes the intestine, forces Qi, reduces moisture.
Cooking time approx. 45 min
Calories p. portion: 429
2 portions
Allergens: EGO

### Quantity of ingredients
Chickpeas  1 cup /  120g. .........................................................water
Hijiki  1 table spoon /  7g. .........................................................water
Salt  1 pinch /  0,5g. .................................................................water
Sunflower oil  1 table spoon /  10g. ............................................ earth
Carrot  2 pieces /  160g. ............................................................ earth
Raisins  2 table spoons /  18g. ................................................... earth
Ginger fresh  1/2 teaspoon /  2g. ...............................................metal
Cumin (Caraway seed)  1 pinch /  0,2g. ....................................metal
Lemon juice  1 dash /  1g. ..........................................................wood
Sour cream 15% fat  1 table spoon /  8g. .......................................*
Curcuma  1 pinch /  0,2g. ..............................................................*
Soybean milk  1 dash /  1g. ........................................................ earth
Coriander  1 pinch /  0,2g. ..........................................................metal
Soy sauce  1 dash /  1g. .............................................................water
Rice round grain  1/2 cup /  60g. ...............................................metal
Water  3 cups /  250g. (yes) ....................................................... earth
Salt  1 pinch /  1g. .....................................................................water

### Cooking instructions:
Preparation:
Soak chickpeas in cold water for several hours or overnight.

After that:
Pour soaking water away; put the chickpeas in cold water; Add 1 tbsp Hijiki and cook the chickpeas bite-proof; Add salt at the end of the cooking time.

Separately:
In a hot pan, fry oil, chopped carrots (more than chickpeas), raisins, grated ginger, plenty of cumin and salt until the
 carrots are half cooked; add the chickpeas and sea algae; Add lemon

juice, a little sour cream, turmeric, soy or rice milk; a pinch of cilantro, add some soy sauce; Let it soak for a few minutes over low heat until the carrots are cooked.

Put the round grain rice with the water, salt and cook for about 20 minutes.

## 9.14 Classic ginger chicken with rice wine

warming and nourishing, directs the Qi upwards, forces the libido, against Qi- und Yang-weakness of spleen, heart and kidneys, in lung Qi deficiency, moisture, sensitivity to cold, listlessness.
Cooking time approx. 30 min
Calories p. portion: 357
4 portions
Allergens: GO

### Quantity of ingredients
Butter organic  2 table spoons /  30g. ........................................ earth
Ginger fresh  2 table spoons /  18g. ............................................metal
Salt  1 pinch /  0,5g. ................................................................water
Chicken meat  2 pieces (legs) /  500g. ........................................ wood
Lychee liqueur  1 dash /  2g. ......................................................... fire
Curry  1 pinch /  1g. ................................................................metal
Sake  1 dash /  1g. ................................................................metal
Corn  4 table spoons /  30g. ..................................................... earth
Millet  1/2 cup /  50g. .............................................................. earth
Water  1 1/2 cups /  200g. (yes).................................................. earth
Salt  1 pinch /  g. ...................................................................water
Lettuce  1/2 piece /  100g. .......................................................... fire
Olive oil  1 table spoon /  10g. .................................................. earth
Vinegar (Apple vinegar)  1 teaspoon /  3g. ................................ wood
Water  2 table spoons /  20g. (yes)............................................. earth
Salt  1 pinch /  0,5g. ...............................................................water
Herbs various  1 table spoon /  8g. ...................................................*

### Cooking instructions:
Heat butter in a hot pan (preferably made of cast iron or enamel); sauté chopped ginger (about 1 heaped tablespoons per chicken leg) on low heat; add some salt, chicken and/or other parts of the chicken and roast all around with gentle heat; add Lychee liqueur or maple syrup, add a little curry and fry for a short time; stir in plenty of sake; add corn kernels

(from the glass, health food trade); boil all the ingredients in the sauce for a few minutes,
 until the meat is cooked; season with salt.

This fits: millet, lettuce or lettuce.

## 9.15 Clear ox tail soup with buckthorn fruit

Forces Qi, nourishes the liver blood, good for ocular fibrillation or dry eyes, muscle tension or calf cramps due to blood deficiency.
Cooking time approx. 1-2 hours
Calories p. portion: 217
6 portions
Allergens: O

### Quantity of ingredients
Basic recipe for a beef soup (warming)  4 cup /  1000g. ......................*
Beef Oxtail pieces  1,1 lbs /  500g. ............................................ earth
Shiitake, dried  4-5 pieces /  4g. ............................................... earth
Onion white  1 piece /  60g. ......................................................metal
Sake  2 table spoons /  20g. ......................................................metal
Ginger fresh  1/2 teaspoon /  2g. ...............................................metal
Bocksdorn fruits (Fructus Lycii, Goji, goji berry dried  1 table spoon /  8g. wood

### Cooking instructions:
Soak shiitake mushrooms. Blanch oxtail slices (This removes fat and impurities).
Cook in the beef broth for 1-2 hours.
Then add the spring onions, shiitake mushrooms, rice wine, buckthorn fruits and ginger and simmer gently.

## 9.16 Clear soup from goose

Forces spleen, stomach and lungs, relieves weakness, forces Qi, calms the stomach, gets Qi moving, directs upwards, strengthens spleen and liver, regulates Qi flow, moisturizes, relaxes, builds up Qi, spreads.
Cooking time approx. 2-3 hours
Calories p. portion: 334
6 portions

**Quantity of ingredients**

Goose parts  1,1 lbs /  500g. ..................................................metal
Carrot  1 piece /  100g. ............................................... earth
Onion (shallot)  1 piece /  25g. ................................................metal
Leek  1 piece /  250g. ................................................metal
Parsley  1 Twig /  4g. ................................................. wood
Lovage  1 Twig /  4g. ................................................metal
Chervil  1 pinch /  0,2g. ...................................................*
Water  4 cup /  1000g. (yes) ..................................... earth
Salt  1 pinch /  0,5g. ................................................water

**Cooking instructions:**

Simmer goose pieces with vegetables and herbs for 2-3 hours. Sift through a fine cloth and cool. Degrease and store in the refrigerator.

## 9.17  Coconut rice with cardamom

Forces lungs and spleen, diuretic, forces Qi, protects liver, forces stomach and spleen, forces muscles, reduces moisture, strengthens Qi and Kidney Jing, strengthens Qi of the heart and lungs, quenches thirst.
Cooking time approx. 45 min
Calories p. portion: 266
4 portions
Allergens: GO

**Quantity of ingredients**

Rice long grain rice  1 cup /  120g. ............................................metal
Water  6 cups /  400g. (yes) ..................................... earth
Sugar cane sugar  1 table spoon /  10g. .................................... earth
Cardamom  1 teaspoon /  2g. ...................................................*
Ginger fresh  1/2 teaspoon /  2g. ................................................metal
Butter organic  2 table spoons /  20g. ......................................... earth
Coconut grated  2 table spoons /  16g. ..................................... earth
Cashews  1 table spoon /  8g. .................................................. earth
Raisins  1 table spoon /  8g. ......................................................... earth
Salt  1 pinch /  0,5g. ................................................water
Lemon  1/2 piece /  15g. .......................................... wood
Pumpkin  3/4 lbs /  300g. .......................................... earth
Olive oil  2 table spoons /  20g. ......................................... earth
Coriander  1 pinch /  0,2g. ................................................metal
Pepper (ground)  1 pinch /  0,2g. ................................................metal
Curry  1 pinch /  0,5g. ................................................metal
Water  1/4 cup /  50g. (yes) ..................................... earth

Salt  1 pinch /  0,5g. ............................................................water
Parsley  1 table spoon /  8g. ....................................................wood
Cardamom  1 pinch /  0,2g. ............................................................*
Turmeric (yellow root)  1 pinch /  0,2g. .............................................*

**Cooking instructions:**
Preparation: Soak long grain rice in cold water for 1 hour and drain.

Then: Heat fresh water till it boils; add some whole cane sugar, plenty of ground cardamom or some cardamom pods, grated ginger and the rice into the hot water and cook.
Separately: heat some butter in a hot pot; add grated coconut, cashews and raisins; add the cooked rice and salt; pour lemon juice over it; mix everything and let it pass for a few minutes.

Pumpkin vegetables: heat olive oil in a pan. Steam the pumpkin (cut in cubes), season with cilantro, pepper and curry, simmer with a little water, salt with sea salt, add chopped parsley with cardamom and turmeric, simmer on a
 small fire for about 10 minutes, depending on the pumpkin, the pumpkin should still be firm.

# 9.18  Coconut soup

Forces Qi and blood, is very warming, nourishes Yin, blood and Jing, moisturizes, relaxes, builds up Qi, spreads, gets Qi moving, directs upwards, dissolves stagnation.
Cooking time approx. 20 min
Calories p. portion: 153
6 portions
Allergens: L

**Quantity of ingredients**
Olive oil  2 table spoons /  20g. ................................................. earth
Leek  1 piece /  200g. ...............................................................metal
Onion white  1 small /  40g. .......................................................metal
Basic recipe for a chicken soup (warming)  4 cup /  1000g. ................*
Lime  1/2 juice /  20g. ............................................................... wood
Coconut flakes  2 table spoons /  18g. ...................................... earth
Coconut milk  1 cup /  250g. ...................................................... earth
Pimento  1 pinch /  0,2g. ............................................................metal
Salt (herbal)  1 pinch /  1g. .......................................................water
Lemongrass  1 table spoon /  8g. ...................................................*

**Cooking instructions:**
Pour olive oil into a pan, sauté the leek and onion, add the chicken broth, add the lemon grass, simmer for about 15 minutes, add coconut flakes and coconut milk, allspice and chili, salt with herb salt. Garnish with lemongrass.


## 9.19 Cod soup with tomatoes

Strengthens kidney Qi, strengthens blood and fluids, promotes urination, forces Qi from spleen and kidney, softens, passes downwardly, scatters and move Qi, moisturizes, reduces cold-evil, softens knots, nourishes liver-Yin.
Cooking time approx. 30 min
Calories p. portion: 176
4 portions
Allergens: DLO

**Quantity of ingredients**
Basic recipe for a fish soup  2 cup /  450g. ......................................*
Cod  5/8 lbs - 8oz /  250g. ......................................................water
Onion (shallot)  1 piece /  20g. ...............................................metal
Anise (Common Fennel)  1/2 teaspoon /  1g. ............................. earth
Ginger fresh  1/2 teaspoon /  1g. ............................................metal
Olive oil  1 teaspoon /  3g. ..................................................... earth
Tomato  1 piece /  50g. ............................................................wood
White wine  1/2 cup /  125g. ....................................................wood
Salt  1 pinch /  0,5g. ...............................................................water
Pepper (ground)  1 pinch /  0,2g. ............................................metal
Parsley  1 table spoon (chopped) /  5g. ...................................wood


**Cooking instructions:**
Fry the onion, anise and freshly grated ginger in oil.
Add finely chopped tomatoes and sauté. Add a little wine and fish soup. Simmer gently for 10-15 minutes. Season with salt and pepper; Add the cod pieces and heat gently. Garnish with parsley at the end.

## 9.20 Hummus (Chickpeasmash)

Strengthens spleen and heart, softens, passes downwardly, moisturizes, relaxes, builds up Qi, spreads, nourishes blood, nourishes blood and liver, harmonizes liver and spleen, forces eyesight, preserves the fluids, contracts.
Cooking time approx. 2 hours
Calories p. portion: 542
2 portions
Allergens: N

**Quantity of ingredients**

| | | |
|---|---|---|
| Chickpeas  1 1/2 cups /  240g. | | water |
| Wakame  1 teaspoon (grated) /  2g. | | water |
| Ginger fresh  1/4 teaspoon /  1g. | | metal |
| Rosemary  1 pinch /  0,5g. | | fire |
| Sesame paste (Tahini)  1 table spoon /  10g. | | earth |
| Olive oil  2 table spoons /  20g. | | earth |
| Lemon juice  1 dash /  2g. | | wood |
| Water  upon need /  g. (yes) | | earth |
| Garlic  1 clove (scraped) /  2g. | | metal |
| Parsley  1 teaspoon (chopped) /  2g. | | wood |
| Peppers  1 pinch /  0,2g. | | earth |
| Curcuma  1 pinch /  0,2g. | | * |
| Coriander  1 pinch /  0,2g. | | metal |
| Cardamom  1 pinch /  0,2g. | | * |
| Pepper (ground)  1 pinch /  0,2g. | | metal |
| Salt (herbal)  1/2 teaspoon /  2g. | | water |

**Cooking instructions:**
Soak chickpeas overnight or for at least 6 hours, pour off soaking water, boil in fresh water for about 1 to 1 ½ hours with a little seaweed and ginger, allow to cool.
Seasoning with a few splashes of lemon juice and parsley.
Add the pepper, garlic cut into small pieces or pressed, more or less coriander and cardamom powder, little chilly powder as desired, tahin and olive oil.

Puree all ingredients together. Depending on the consistency, add water. It should be a smooth paste.
Spread on cereal, crackers or toasted bread or enjoy with salad.

## 9.21 Indian Dal soup

Reduces internal heat and moisture, softens, passes downwardly, strengthens spleen and liver, regulates Qi flow, moisturizes, relaxes, builds up Qi, spreads, forces liver and kidney, reduces damp heat.
Cooking time approx. 30 min
Calories p. portion: 256
2 portions
Allergens: EN

**Quantity of ingredients**
Lentils  3/8 lbs - 6oz /  175g. .....................................................water
Sesame oil  2 table spoons /  30g. ............................................ earth
Carrot  1 piece /  100g. .............................................................. earth
Onion (shallot)  1 piece /  15g. ...................................................metal
Water  1 1/2 cups /  200g. (yes)................................................. earth
Ginger fresh  2 slices /  1g. .......................................................metal
Salt  1 pinch /  0,5g. ..................................................................water
Soy sauce  1 teaspoon /  3g. .....................................................water
Parsley  1 teaspoon (chopped) /  3g. ........................................ wood
Thyme  1 teaspoon /  3g. ...................................................................*
Basil  1 table spoon /  5g. ..........................................................metal

**Cooking instructions:**
Soak the lentils overnight.
in a hot pot, carrot, onion and a little ginger fry, pour water. Add the lentils and cook until soft. Add salt or soy sauce and cook for another 10 minutes.
Stir in parsley before serving; Sprinkle thyme or basil over it.
Variant: Other herbs such as sage, rosemary or lovage allow a variety of flavors.

## 9.22 Japanese algae soup

Strengthens spleen and liver, regulates Qi flow, moisturizes, relaxes, builds up Qi, spreads, nourishes the lungs
 and spleen, distributes mucus, dissolves mucus, dissolves stagnation, directs upwards, gets Qi moving und Yang.
Cooking time approx. 20 min
Calories p. portion: 47
3 portions

**Quantity of ingredients**

Wakame  1 oz /  25g. ..............................................................water
Water  2 cup /  450g. (yes)......................................................earth
Onion (shallot)  1-2 pcs. /  30g. ..............................................metal
Radish (white, green, purple-red)  1/8 lbs - 2oz /  50g. ...............metal
Carrot  2 pieces /  180g. .........................................................earth
Miso  2 table spoons /  20g. ....................................................water
Parsley  2 table spoons /  20g. ................................................wood
Onion (spring onion)  1 table spoon (sliced)..............................metal

**Cooking instructions:**
Soak wakame in water for a few minutes, remove and bring the water to the boil. Add finely chopped onions and wakame, radishes and carrots, cut into thin strips, and simmer for another 10 minutes. Dissolve miso in a little cooled cooking water and add it at the end. Sprinkle with parsley and spring onions.

## 9.23 Kidney bean pot with lamb and sage

Nourishes Yin from heart and kidney, strengthens spleen and kidney Yang, forces Qi, heats middle and lower heater, dissolves stagnation, directs upwards, moisturizes, relaxes, builds up Qi, spreads.
Cooking time approx. 1 1/2 hours
Calories p. portion: 391
4 portions
Allergens: F

**Quantity of ingredients**

Soybean oil  2 table spoons /  30g. ...........................................earth
Onion white  2 pieces /  120g. .................................................metal
Lamb meat  5/8 oz /  200g. ......................................................fire
Salt  1 pinch /  0,5g. ................................................................water
Sage  4-5 leaves /  2g. .............................................................fire
Rosemary  1/2 teaspoon /  2g. .................................................fire
Thyme  1/2 teaspoon /  2g. ...........................................................*
Kidney beans (red)  5/8 lbs - 8oz /  250g. ...............................water
Water  3 cups /  750g. (yes) ....................................................earth

**Cooking instructions:**
Soak kidney beans in water overnight and strain.
In a saucepan with oil, roast the onion. Dice the lamb and place in the pot.
Season with salt, sage, rosemary and thyme.

Roast lamb well and cover pot. Cook over low heat and add ten-quarters of a gallon (750ml.) of cold water after 10 minutes.
Salt again.
Heat till it boils. Add beans to it.
Simmer for at least 1 hour until the beans and meat are tender.

## 9.24 Kudzu soup in the morning

Moisturizes, relaxes, builds up Qi, spreads, forces stomach, harmonizes middle, reduces internal heat, detoxifies, softens, passes downwardly.
Cooking time approx. 5 min
Calories p. portion: 12
1 portions
Allergens: E

### Quantity of ingredients
Water  1 cup /  250g. (yes) ......................................................... earth
Soy sauce  1 dash /  2g. ............................................................water
Umeboshi paste  1 knife tip /  2g. ...............................................water

### Cooking instructions:
Mix kudzu with cold water and heat till it boils while stirring. Once it is glassy, remove from heat and let cool. Season
 with Tamari and Umeboshipaste or crushed umeboshi plums

There is always the possibility to support your stomach and intestines with this recipe, taken before the right breakfast.
A morning cure for stomach and mucous membranes. Fix the base balance.

## 9.25 Lamb leg in the oven

Strengthens spleen and kidney Yang, relieves weakness, forces Qi, heats middle and lower heater, forces Qi, forces spleen, relieves inflammation, moisturizes, relaxes, builds up Qi, spreads, nourishes liver-Yin, cools heat, produces humors.
Cooking time approx. 2 hours
Calories p. portion: 484
6 portions

**Quantity of ingredients**

Lamb meat  2,2 lbs (leg) /  1000g. ................................................ fire
Olive oil  2 table spoons /  20g. ................................................ earth
Potato  1,1 lbs /  500g. ................................................ earth
Onion (shallot)  3 pieces /  50g. ................................................metal
Pepper (ground)  1 pinch /  0,2g. ................................................metal
Salt  1 pinch /  0,5g. ................................................water
Tomato  4-5 pieces /  200g. ................................................ wood
Pepper powder (hot)  1 pinch /  0,5g. ................................................ fire
Rosemary  1 pinch /  0,2g. ................................................ fire
Thyme  1 pinch /  0,2g. ................................................*
Savory  1 teaspoon /  1g. ................................................water

**Cooking instructions:**
Put the leg of lamb on a baking tray painted with olive oil.

Distribute peeled and quartered potatoes and the quartered onions on the plate.

Sprinkle with pepper, salt; add tomatoes roughly cut; dust with rose paprika; drizzle with olive oil; sprinkle dried rosemary, savory, thyme over it.

Bake at 250°C/482°F for 15 minutes; then reduce the heat to 150°C/302°F and bake for another 1 1/2 hours; occasionally drizzle some water over.

This fits: dry red wine, endive, radicchio, corn salad and millet.

# 9.26  Lamb soup HARIRA

Forces Qi and Yang, is very warming, nourishes liver-Yin, produces humors, strengthens spleen and kidney Yang, relieves weakness, forces Qi, heats middle and lower heater.
Cooking time approx. 1 hour
Calories p. portion: 205
6 portions
Allergens: ACO

**Quantity of ingredients**

| Ingredient | Amount | Element |
|---|---|---|
| Lamb meat | 5/8 lbs - 8oz / 250g. | fire |
| Tomato | 3 big / 250g. | wood |
| Onion white | 2 pieces / 120g. | metal |
| Parsley | 1 Bunch / 100g. | wood |
| Ginger fresh | 1/2 teaspoon / 2g. | metal |
| Curcuma | 2 1/2 teaspoon / 2g. | * |
| Salt | 1 teaspoon / 2g. | water |
| Pepper (ground) | 1 pinch / 0,2g. | metal |
| Basic recipe for a beef soup (warming) | 4 cup / 950g. | * |
| Noodles (whole grain) with egg | 1/8 lbs - 2oz (small) / g. | wood |
| Chicken egg | 2 pieces / 120g. | earth |
| Lemon juice | 2 teaspoons / 8g. | wood |
| Cinnamon ground | 1 pinch / 0,2g. | * |

**Cooking instructions:**

Cut the meat into 3cm strips. Peel Tomato and cut into pieces. (Leave seeds) Finely dice the onions. Chop parsley. Heat the oil, fry the meat. Add ginger, turmeric and salt. Then add the tomato, onion and the parsley and pour in the hot meat stock. Cover the soup and cook for 45 minutes over a low heat. Add the noodles, heat till it boils and cook for 10 minutes with the pot open. Cook over a low heat. Remove the pot from the oven. Mix the eggs with the lemon juice and cinnamon and stir in the soup. Do not cook anymore.

## 9.27 Leek soup with almond mash

Gets Qi moving, moisten the lungs and large intestine, cools heat, preserves the fluids, contracts, forces Qi, forces spleen, relieves inflammation, moisturizes, relaxes, spreads.
Cooking time approx. 20 min
Calories p. portion: 115
4 portions
Allergens: HN

**Quantity of ingredients**

| Ingredient | Amount | Element |
|---|---|---|
| Water | 2 cup / 480g. (yes) | earth |
| Sugar cane sugar | 1 pinch / 0,3g. | earth |
| Leek | 2 pieces / 400g. | metal |
| Salt | 1 pinch / 0,5g. | water |
| Lemon juice | 1/2 piece / 15g. | wood |
| Rosemary | 1 Twig / 3g. | fire |
| Pepper powder (hot) | Alternative to rosemary / g. | fire |

Potato flour  1 table spoon / 8g. ................................................. earth
Almond puree  2 table spoons / 20g. ......................................... earth
Sesame oil  few drops / 1g. ....................................................... earth
Pepper white (ground)  1 pinch / 0,2g. ........................................metal

## Cooking instructions:

Add a pinch of sugar to hot water, add chopped leeks and a pinch of salt; simmer until the leek is half cooked; season with lemon juice, fresh rosemary or rose paprika.

Dissolve potato flour separately in cold water; thicken the soup with it.

Add almond purée, a few drops of toasted sesame oil, pepper and simmer until the leek is cooked.

Variant:
Add mushrooms; they build up juices and soften the yangling effect of the leeks.

# 9.28 Legumes

Strengthens spleen and liver, regulates Qi flow, moisturizes, relaxes, builds up Qi, spreads, nourishes blood and Qi, diuretic, harmonizes Qi (in the middle and lower heater), detoxifies, reduces internal heat and moisture.
Cooking time approx. 30 min
Calories p. portion: 31
5 portions

## Quantity of ingredients

Pinto beans speckled  1/4 lbs - 4oz / 100g. ...............................water
Lentils  1/8 lbs - 2oz / 50g. .......................................................water
Peas, green  1/8 lbs - 2oz / 50g. ...............................................water
Water  4 cup / 1000g. (yes) ...................................................... earth
Lemon  1 slice / 2g. ................................................................. wood
Juniper berry  6 pieces / 2g. ........................................................ fire
Thyme  1 Twig / 3g. ....................................................................... *
Rosemary  1 Twig / 3g. ................................................................ fire
Carrot  1 piece / 100g. ............................................................. earth
Savory  1-2 teaspoons / 5g. .....................................................water
Ginger fresh  a great piece / 3g. ...............................................metal
Bay leaf  2-3 leaves / 1g. .............................................................. *
Wakame  1-2 strips / 1g. ..........................................................water

**Cooking instructions:**
Legumes such as beans, lentils, peas or chickpeas are soaked in plenty of cold water for several hours to three days. The water should be changed every 8 hours. Then pour off soaking water and wash legumes thoroughly.

Preparation:
Cook the legumes with fresh cold water and a slice of ginger and bring to froth. Cook without lid for about 5 minutes, scooping off the foam. Only then add the following ingredients: a slice of lemon or lemon juice, crush juniper berries, thyme; (possibly 1 knife tip of asafetida in case of severe indigestion). Add savory, sage, juniper, fenugreek seeds, carrots, bay leaves, fresh ginger, wakame algae.

Simmer on the slightest flame until beans or lentils have the desired consistency.
This base can be stored for 3-4 days in the refrigerator.


## 9.29  Lentils and rice stew

Strengthens spleen and liver, regulates Qi flow, moisturizes, relaxes, builds up Qi, spreads, warms the stomach
 and spleen, harmonizes the intestine, forces Qi, reduces moisture, brings the liver Qi in motion, cools heat.
Cooking time approx. 25 min
Calories p. portion: 232
3 portions
Allergens: LNO


**Quantity of ingredients**
Lentils  1/4 lbs - 4oz /  100g. .......................................................water
Water  5 cups /  500g. (yes) ...................................................... earth
Rice variety any  1 cup /  120g. ...............................................metal
Sesame oil  1 table spoon /  10g. .............................................. earth
Carrot  2 pieces /  150g. ........................................................... earth
Celery sticks  2 rods /  20g. ...................................................... earth
Cumin (Caraway seed)  1 pinch /  0,2g. ...................................metal
Salt  1 pinch /  0,5g. .................................................................water
Vinegar (Apple vinegar)  1 dash /  2g. ...................................... wood
Parsley  2 table spoons /  18g.  ................................................ wood

**Cooking instructions:**
Soak the dry lentils the day before.
Heat sesame oil in a hot pot; cut carrot and celery into small pieces and sauté; add rice, a pinch of cumin and lentils
and heat till it boils.
If the lenses are soft, add salt; season with a little vinegar and garnish with parsley.

Variant: In summer you can omit the cumin and add fresh green peas, Chinese cabbage or celery.

## 9.30 Marinated turkey with cashew nuts from the wok

Warming and nourishing, directs the Qi upwards, forces Qi, blood and Yang, dissolves stagnation, warms the stomach and spleen, harmonizes the intestine, forces Qi, reduces moisture.
Cooking time approx. 30 min
Calories p. portion: 319
4 portions
Allergens: ELNO

**Quantity of ingredients**
Turkey breast meat  3/4 lbs /  300g. ......................................... earth
Sake  until covered /  g. ...........................................................metal
Sesame oil  2 table spoons /  30g. ............................................. earth
Ginger fresh  1/2 teaspoon /  2g. ...............................................metal
Salt  1 pinch /  0,5g. ................................................................water
Lemon  1/2 piece /  15g. ........................................................... wood
Red wine  1/2 cup /  125g. .......................................................... fire
Sugar cane sugar  1 pinch /  1g. ................................................ earth
Onion (spring onion)  4 pieces /  80g. .......................................metal
Tomato  2 pieces /  100g. .......................................................... wood
Basic recipe for a chicken soup (warming)  1 cup /  120g. .................*
Cashews  2 table spoons /  16g. ................................................ earth
Soy sauce  1 dash /  2g. ...........................................................water
Rice Basmati  1 cup /  120g. ......................................................metal
Water  6 cups /  400g. (yes) ....................................................... earth
Salt  1 pinch /  0,5g. ................................................................water

**Cooking instructions:**
Preparation: cover sliced turkey meat with rice wine; marinate overnight or for a few hours.

Then: strain and drain well; heat sesame oil in a hot wok; fry finely chopped ginger; sauté the meat for a short time;
 add the marinade; add salt, lemon juice, red wine or rose paprika; let the meat soak in the sauce for 2 - 3 minutes; then exhaust it; add some sugar to the sauce in the wok; add a few spring onions (the white parts), a pinch of salt, chopped tomatoes, 1 cup of chicken broth; simmer so that the onions are still crisp.
Roasted cashews, add the cashews and the meat to the sauce and heat; season with soy sauce; stir in the green of the chopped green onions.
Boil the rice with the water, salt and cook for about 20 minutes.

## 9.31 Millet with egg and butter

Forces blood, Yin and Jing, nourishes Yin, moisturizes in case of internal dryness, forces blood, forces spleen, calms nerves and stomach, strengthens spleen and kidney, diuretic, strengthens Qi and kidney Jing, moisturizes, relaxes, builds up Qi, spreads.
Cooking time approx. 25 min
Calories p. portion: 338
2 portions
Allergens: CG

**Quantity of ingredients**
Millet  1 cup /  100g. .................................................................. earth
Ginger fresh  1/2 teaspoon /  1g. .............................................. metal
Salt  1 pinch /  0,5g. ................................................................. water
Parsley  2 table spoons /  16g. ................................................. wood
Pepper powder (hot)  1 pinch /  1g. ............................................. fire
Chicken egg  2 pieces /  100g. ................................................. earth
Butter organic  2 table spoons /  20g. ....................................... earth
Nutmeg  1 pinch /  0,2g. ........................................................... metal
Water  1 1/2 cups /  200g. (yes)................................................. earth

**Cooking instructions:**
Simmer the millet with the ginger and nutmeg in the water for 5 min. and let it swell for another 30 min.
Cook and peel 1 soft egg per person; pile up the millet on plates and place 1 egg each in a hollow in the millet mountain; Put butterflakes over it. Sprinkle with chopped parsley and the rose paprika.

## 9.32 Minestrone

Forces Qi of the middle, cools heat, diuretic, cools blood, reduces mucus, reduces heat, moisturizes, relaxes, builds up Qi, spreads. nourishes liver-Yin, cools heat, produces humors.
Cooking time approx. 30 min
Calories p. portion: 211
4 portions
Allergens: GL

**Quantity of ingredients**
Onion (shallot)  2 pieces /  40g. ................................................metal
Sunflower oil  1 teaspoon /  10g. ................................................ earth
Water  2 cup /  480g. (yes)........................................................ earth
Carrot  2 pieces /  120g. ............................................................ earth
Savoy cabbage / kale  Handful /  15g. ...................................... earth
Beans (green, fresh)  Handful /  20g. .........................................water
Celery sticks  3 pieces /  20g. ................................................... earth
Peas, green  4 table spoons /  30g. ...........................................water
Zucchini  1 piece /  200g. ........................................................... earth
Rice variety any  1 cup /  120g. ..................................................metal
Bay leaf  3 leaves /  1g. ....................................................................*
Sunflower oil  1 table spoon /  10g. ........................................... earth
Salt  1 pinch /  1g. .....................................................................water
Tomato  3 pieces /  150g. ........................................................... wood
Thyme  1 Twig /  3g. .........................................................................*
Parmesan  2 table spoons /  18g. .............................................. earth
Basil  4 leaves /  2g. ..................................................................metal

**Cooking instructions:**
Fry the onion in oil in a glassy saucepan and add water. Add vegetables, rice and salt and simmer gently. If the vegetables are firm, add tomatoes, a small sprig of thyme, basil and bay leaf and leave to simmer. Serve with Parmesan.

## 9.33 Mung bean stew

Dissipates excess heat, is very nutritious, reduces heat and poison, softens, passes downwardly, warms the stomach and spleen, harmonizes the intestine, forces Qi, reduces moisture.
Cooking time approx. 2 hours
Calories p. portion: 665
2 portions

**Quantity of ingredients**

Mung bean  5/8 lbs - 8oz - 500g / 300g. .....................................water
Sunflower oil  2 table spoons / 30g. .......................................... earth
Amaranth  1/2 teaspoon / 2g. ..................................................... fire
Fennel seeds ground  1/2 teaspoon / 2g. ................................. earth
Cumin (Caraway seed)  1/2 teaspoon / 2g. ...............................metal
Coriander  1/2 teaspoon / 2g. ...................................................metal
Rice round grain  1/2 cup / 60g. ...............................................metal
Water  3 cups / 300g. (yes) ....................................................... earth
Ginger fresh  1 inch / 3g. ..........................................................metal
Kombu seaweed (Saccharina japonica)  1 inch / 2g. .................water
Salt  1 pinch / 0,5g. ..................................................................water
Parsley  1 table spoon / 3g. ..................................................... wood

**Cooking instructions:**

Soak mung beans overnight.
Heat sunflower oil in a hot pot. Stir in the amaranth, fennel seeds, cumin and coriander and fry briefly.
admit basmati rice, some ginger and mung beans and roast briefly.
Pour water and heat till it boils.
Add a piece of kombu alga and salt.
Simmer for 1-1/2 hours.
Garnish with parsley or coriander.

## 9.34  Pea dish

Strengthens the middle, diuretic, harmonizes Qi (in the middle and lower heater), detoxifies, softens, passes downwardly, forces blood, Yin and Jing, nourishes Yin, moisturizes in case of internal dryness.
Cooking time approx. 1-2 hours
Calories p. portion: 406
1 portions
Allergens: CE

**Quantity of ingredients**

Peas  3/8 lbs - 6oz (dried) / 150g. .............................................water
Lemon  1 piece / 40g. ............................................................... wood
Juniper berry  6 pieces / 2g. ...................................................... fire
Sunflower oil  1 teaspoon / 3g. ................................................ earth
Pepper white (ground)  1 pinch / 0,3g. ......................................metal
Bay leaf  3 leaves / 2g. ................................................................. *
Onion white  1 piece / 50g. .......................................................metal

Thyme  1 teaspoon /  2g. ..................................................................*
Ginger fresh  1/2 teaspoon /  1g. ..............................................metal
Chicken egg  1 piece /  60g. .................................................... earth
Wakame  1 inch /  2g. ..............................................................water
Salt  1 pinch /  1g. ....................................................................water
Soy sauce  per taste /  2g. .......................................................water

**Cooking instructions:**
Soak dried peas in plenty of cold water for several hours or overnight.
Pour away soaking water and wash peas thoroughly.

Place the peas with about 1 1/2 l of cold water and heat till it boils; cook
without lid for 5 minutes; scoop up the foam that forms; only then add the
following ingredients: a slice of lemon, juniper berries, oil, peppercorns,
bay leaves, chopped onion, dried thyme, chopped ginger, simmer about 2
strips of wakame or 1 tbsp Hijiki with lid closed for 1 - 2 hours; After 1
hour, try if the peas are already soft, because the cooking time changes
with the soaking time and the age of aging; when the peas are cooked,
remove the lemon slice, juniper berries and peppercorns; with salt, soy
sauce, lemon juice to taste.

Note: The dish can be refrigerated for 3-4 days and heated in portions.

Serve with: crispy vegetables, rice or millet steamed in water.


## 9.35 Plums with curd cheese

Preserves the fluids, contracts.
Cooking time approx. 10 min
Calories p. portion: 141
2 portions
Allergens: G


**Quantity of ingredients**
Plums  1 lbs /  500g. ................................................................wood
Butter organic  1/2 teaspoon /  2g. ............................................ earth
Vanilla  1 pinch /  0,2g. .................................................................*
Cinnamon ground  1 pinch /  0,2g. ...................................................*
Coriander  1 pinch /  0,2g. ........................................................metal
Cardamom  1 pinch /  0,2g. ...........................................................*

Lemon juice  1 dash /  1g. ........................................................... wood
Cocoa  1 pinch /  0,3g. .................................................... fire
Apple juice (natural cloudy)  1 dash /  3g. ................... earth
Sugar cane sugar  1 teaspoon /  3g. ........................... earth
Curd cheese 20%  2 table spoons /  30g. ......................................... *

**Cooking instructions:**
Cut plums in half. Steam the plums in a pan in a little butter. Add vanilla, cinnamon and a pinch of cilantro and cardamom.
Add water so that the plums ¼ are covered.
Add lemon juice and a pinch of cocoa. Pour with little pear or apple juice, so that the plums are covered about halfway.
Sweet to taste with whole cane sugar.
Approximately Simmer for 7 minutes on the lightest heat so that the plums are tender but not overcooked.
Arrange plums in a circle on the plate.
In the middle a tablespoon of organic quark (who may like to use sheep milk quark).
Pour little juice of cooked plums over the dessert.

# 9.36  Polenta with fried egg

Nourishing and slightly warming, builds up Qi, forces blood, Yin and Jing, strengthens stomach Qi, diuretic, moisturizes, relaxes, builds up Qi, spreads, gets Qi moving, forces fluids production, reduces cold-evil.
Not: in wet heat of the gallbladder.
Cooking time approx. 15 min
Calories p. portion: 410
2 portions
Allergens: CG

**Quantity of ingredients**
Water  1 1/2 cups /  200g. (yes).................................................... earth
Corn Grease (Polenta)  1 cup /  120g. ......................................... earth
Ginger fresh  1 pinch /  0,5g. .................................................... metal
Butter organic  1/2 teaspoon /  2g. .............................................. earth
Pepper (ground)  1 pinch /  0,2g. ................................................ metal
Nutmeg  1 pinch /  0,2g. .......................................................... metal
Salt  1 pinch /  0,5g. ................................................................ water

Lemon juice  1 dash /  1g. ...........................................................wood
Pepper powder (hot)  1 pinch /  0,3g. .............................................. fire
Chicken egg  4 pieces /  250g.  ................................................. earth
Chives  2 table spoons /  14g.  .................................................metal

## Cooking instructions:

Stir in a saucepan with hot water polenta and a little ginger; swell until the polenta is cooked.

Add a piece of butter, pepper, nutmeg, salt, a few drops of lemon, a pinch of rose paprika.

Put the polenta in a fireproof bowl.

Put 1 fried egg per person on top; bake in the oven for a few minutes, so that the egg yolk is still liquid.

Sprinkle with ground pepper, finely chopped chives and a little salt.

# 9.37 Polenta with ratatouille

Strengthens stomach Qi, diuretic, moisturizes, relaxes, builds up Qi, spreads, nourishes liver-Yin, cools heat, produces humors, cools and moves blood, reduces external and internal wind, reduces internal heat.
Cooking time approx. 30 min
Calories p. portion: 226
4 portions
Allergens: G

## Quantity of ingredients

Corn Grease (Polenta)  1 cup /  120g. ...................................... earth
Water  1 1/2 cups /  240g. (yes)..................................................... earth
Aubergine  1 piece (large) /  200g. ............................................. earth
Zucchini  2 pieces /  500g. ......................................................... earth
Onion white  2 pieces /  120g. ....................................................metal
Tomato  2 pieces (blended) /  200g. ...........................................wood
Olive oil  2 table spoons /  20g. ................................................. earth
Salt  1 pinch /  0,5g. .................................................................water
Parsley  1 table spoon (chopped) /  8g. ......................................wood
Thyme  1/2 teaspoon /  1g. ............................................................ *
Onion (spring onion)  2 table spoons (chopped) /  12g. ...............metal
Basil  4 leaves /  2g. .................................................................metal
Parmesan  2 table spoons /  20g. ............................................. earth

**Cooking instructions:**
Use double the amount of water to polenta, add salt and oil and heat till it boils. Stir in polenta, stirring constantly. Take off the fire and let it swell for 20 minutes. Meanwhile, cut the onion, fry in a saucepan with hot oil. Add the diced zucchini, tomatoes and melanzani and simmer for about 20 minutes. Add basil, thyme, salt.
Coat baking tray with oil, apply polenta evenly and wait until it gets stronger.
Add the cooked ratatouille to polenta, portion and then put in the oven for a few minutes (possibly with grated parmesan).
Sprinkle with fresh parsley and finely chopped spring onion.
The valuable tip: The Polenta sections are ideal for on the go.

## 9.38 Quick flakes with compote or jam

Forces Qi, dries out, passes downwardly, strengthens middle heater, moisturizes, relaxes, builds up Qi, spreads, strengthens kidney Qi, essence and brain, forces kidney, warms the middle.
Cooking time approx. 5 min
Calories p. portion: 189
2 portions
Allergens: H

**Quantity of ingredients**
Quinoa  5-7 table spoons /  50g. ..................................................... fire
Water  1 cup /  250g. (yes) ......................................................... earth
Compote (fruits of the season)  1 cup /  100g.  ............................... *
Walnuts  1 table spoon (grated) /  8g.  ..................................... earth
Olive oil  1 table spoon /  10g.  ................................................. earth
Honey  2 table spoons /  20g.  .................................................. earth
Vanilla  1 pinch /  0,2g.  .............................................................. *
Anise (Common Fennel)  1 pinch /  0,2g.  .................................. earth
Cardamom  1 pinch /  0,2g.  ........................................................ *

**Cooking instructions:**
Put the quinoa flakes in a pan and add water. Boil for 3-5 minutes, pull from the fire, add nuts and compote. Add a dash of oil. Sweeten as needed with honey, whole cane sugar or agave syrup.

Spices and aromas: vanilla, anise, fennel or coriander, cardamom, a little chili.
Winter: apple compote, pear compote, fruit jam.
Summer: plum compote, apricot compote.

## 9.39 Quinoa piquant with avocado

Nourishes Yin from liver, lungs and colon, moisturizes, relaxes, builds up Qi, spreads, strengthens spleen and liver, regulates Qi flow, moisturizes, relaxes, builds up Qi, spreads, forces Qi, dries out, regulates Qi, warms spleen and kidney, dissolves stagnation
Cooking time approx. 20 min
Calories p. portion: 561
2 portions

**Quantity of ingredients**
Water  1 1/2 cups /  240g. (yes)................................................. earth
Quinoa  1 cup /  100g. ................................................................ fire
Carrot  1 piece shredded /  100g. ............................................. earth
Onion (spring onion)  2 table spoons (chopped) /  12g. ...............metal
Curcuma  1/2 teaspoon /  1g. .........................................................*
Avocado  1 piece soft /  300g. ................................................. earth
Salt  1 pinch /  0,5g. ................................................................water
Pepper (ground)  1 pinch /  0,2g. ............................................metal
Linseed oil  2 teaspoons /  4g. ................................................ earth

**Cooking instructions:**
Put quinoa in hot water.
Add grated carrot, pepper and salt, finely chopped spring onion and turmeric.
Simmer about 20 minutes, pull from the fire.
Add pre-cut avocado.
Add a dash of oil and sprinkle with fresh parsley and gomasio.
Spices and herbs: turmeric, cardamom, cress, parsley, chives.
Variation: For those who want more hearty, you can also use a sardine from organic fish preserves. If you are the "protein type", this breakfast will hold on for a long time!


## 9.40 Quinoa with peach

Strengthens blood and fluids, brings blood into motion, builds up Qi, spreads, forces Qi, dries out, passes downwardly, strengthens middle heater, moisturizes.
Cooking time approx. 20 min
Calories p. portion: 248
2 portions

**Quantity of ingredients**
Quinoa  1 cup /  100g. ................................................................ fire
Water  1 1/2 cups /  240g. (yes)................................................. earth
Honey  2 teaspoons /  4g. ........................................................ earth
Peaches  2 pieces /  240g. ....................................................... earth
Linseed oil  2 teaspoons /  4g. ................................................. earth
Lemon Balm (fresh)  1 teaspoon (chopped) /  1g. ......................metal
Cinnamon ground  1 pinch /  0,2g. ...............................................*
Vanilla  1 pinch /  0,2g. ...............................................................*

**Cooking instructions:**
In the evening: Put quinoa in hot water and boil soft, covered 15 to 20 minutes.
In the morning: Warm up quinoa with 1 tablespoon water.
Steam lightly Peaches in a saucepan or add them fresh. Decorate with fresh lemon balm.

Summer: nectarines, apricots
Winter: Pickled fruit, pear, apples

# 9.41 Radish with horseradish

Slightly refreshing and moisturizing, dissolves stagnation, nourishes blood and liver, harmonizes liver and spleen, forces eyesight, preserves the fluids, contracts, nourishes the lungs and spleen, distributes mucus, dissolves mucus, dissolves stagnation, directs upwards.
Cooking time approx. 30 min
Calories p. portion: 196
2 portions
Allergens: GNO

**Quantity of ingredients**
Butter organic  1 table spoon /  8g. ............................................ earth
Radish (white, green, purple-red)  1/2 piece /  50g. ....................metal
Water  2 table spoons /  10g. (yes)............................................ earth
Lemon juice  2 table spoons /  20g. ...........................................wood
White wine  2 table spoons /  20g. .............................................wood
Pepper powder (hot)  1 pinch /  0,2g. .......................................... fire
Sesame oil  1 teaspoon /  3g. .................................................... earth
Radish horseradish  2 table spoons /  20g. ...............................metal

Salt  1 pinch /  0,5g. ................................................................water
Parsley  1 Bunch (chopped) /  80g. ...........................................wood
Rice long grain rice  1/2 cup /  60g. .........................................metal
Water  3 cups /  300g. (yes) ..................................................... earth
Salt  1 pinch /  0,5g. ................................................................water

**Cooking instructions:**
In a hot pan melt the butter, sautéed into stripes cut radish. Add cold
water, lemon juice, white wine, a pinch of rose paprika and stir in the
sesame oil; with 2 - 3 tablespoons fresh grated horseradish (alternatively
1 teaspoon from the glass), salt to taste; Sprinkle with chopped parsley.

Place the rice with the water, salt and cook for about 15 minutes.


## 9.42 Radish with spring onions and carrots

Nutritious, moisturizing and dynamizing, moves Qi and blood, dissolves
stagnation, directs upwards, strengthens stomach Qi, diuretic,
moisturizes, relaxes, builds up Qi, spreads. regulates Qi, warms spleen
and kidney.
Cooking time approx. 30 min
Calories p. portion: 246
2 portions
Allergens: EG


**Quantity of ingredients**
Carrot  2 pieces /  200g. ......................................................... earth
Radish black  1/2 piece /  100g. ...............................................metal
Ginger powder  1 knife tip /  0,2g. ............................................metal
Onion (spring onion)  1 piece /  20g. .........................................metal
Salt  1 pinch /  0,5g. ................................................................water
Soy sauce  1 dash /  2g. ..........................................................water
Lemon juice  2 table spoons /  16g. ..........................................wood
Curcuma  1 pinch /  0,2g. ...............................................................*
Pepper powder (hot)  1 pinch /  0,2g. ........................................ fire
Butter organic  1 teaspoon /  3g. .............................................. earth
Water  1 cup /  250g. (yes) ...................................................... earth
Corn Grease (Polenta)  1 cup /  100g. ...................................... earth
Salt  1 pinch /  0,5g. ................................................................water

**Cooking instructions:**
Cook finely chopped carrots, black or white finely chopped radish, a pinch of grated ginger. Steam for 10 minutes, then strain.
In the meantime stir in chopped spring onions, salt, soy sauce, a little lemon juice, a pinch of turmeric or rose paprika and a piece of butter.

Garnish:
Stir the polenta into a pot of hot water, stirring constantly, until the polenta has the desired texture. Pull the polenta off the fire and let it swell for about 10 minutes.

## 9.43 Red lentils with avocado and radish

Nutritious and moisturizing builds up Qi and fluids, drives sweat, reduces blood fat, stimulates, dissolves stagnation.
Cooking time approx. 20 min
Calories p. portion: 269
3 portions
Allergens: N

**Quantity of ingredients**
Ginger fresh  2 slices /  2g. .......................................................metal
Water  1 1/2 cups /  200g. (yes)................................................. earth
Lentils red  1 cup peeled /  100g. .................................................water
Wakame  1 inch /  1g. ................................................................water
Salt  1 pinch /  0,5g. .................................................................water
Lemon juice  1 dash /  1g. ........................................................ wood
Curcuma  1 pinch /  0,3g. ................................................................*
Avocado  1 piece /  300g. ........................................................ earth
Pepper (ground)  1 pinch /  0,2g. ................................................metal
Pepper powder (hot)  1 pinch /  0,2g. ............................................ fire
Sesame oil  1 dash /  1g. .......................................................... earth
Radish (white, green, purple-red)  1 cup /  100g. ........................metal

**Cooking instructions:**
Put in a pot with water, some chopped ginger, peeled red lentils, a piece of wakame or a small amount of hijiki and simmer until the lentils are soft. Season with salt, lemon juice and turmeric.

Meanwhile: place half an avocado per serving on one-third of the plate: add ground pepper, a pinch of salt, a little lemon juice, a pinch of sweet pepper and a little sesame oil.

Put the grated radish on the second plate third.

Fill the lentil dish into the last third of the plate.
Variant: Use radish slices instead of radishes.

## 9.44 Reissue soup with fresh fruits

Forces kidney and bladder, strengthens Qi and kidney Jing, moisturizes, relaxes, builds up Qi, reduces internal heat, produces humors, moisturizes, spreads, expels cold, dissolves stagnation, drives sweat, stimulates nerves.
Cooking time approx. 1 1/2 hours
Calories p. portion: 143
4 portions
Allergens: G

**Quantity of ingredients**
Rice wild (nature rice) 1 cup / 100g. .........................................metal
Water 8 cups / 900g. (yes).................................................... earth
Apple (sweet) 1 1/2 cups / 200g. ............................................ earth
Butter organic 1 table spoon / 10g. ........................................ earth
Vanilla 1 pinch / 0,2g. ..................................................................*
Sugar cane sugar 2 teaspoons / 6g. ........................................ earth

**Cooking instructions:**
Prepare rice congee according to basic recipe.

At the end, add finely chopped fruits to the season, vanilla, chili and butter; sweet to taste.

Variant: With nuts, the dish can always be made richer and more filling.
Effect: Cooked or steamed fruits are easier to digest and act better than raw. For some fruits, which are particularly suitable for hot summer days - such as melons and berries - it is still advisable to add the fruits only to a hot porridge.
Other types of fruit - such as apples, pears, plums and cherries - can also be simmered for a while.

## 9.45 Rice congee with crushed walnuts

Nourishing and slightly warming, warms the middle, builds up Qi, warms the stomach and spleen, harmonizes the intestine, forces Qi, reduces moisture.
Cooking time approx. 2 hours and more
Calories p. portion: 406
2 portions
Allergens: H

**Quantity of ingredients**
Basic recipe for a rice soup (Congee)  4 cups / 500g. ......................*
Sugar cane sugar  2 table spoons / 20g. .................................. earth
Walnuts  1 cup / 70g. .............................................. earth
Cinnamon ground  1 pinch / 0,2g. ...................................*

**Cooking instructions:**
Cook the basic recipe for rice soup (congee)
Note: The crushed walnuts can be cooked from the beginning.
Variation: Refine with sweet or spicy ingredients as you like. In particular, cinnamon, cloves, and ginger increase the warming effect and wholesomeness.


## 9.46 Rice congee with dried fruit

Warms the stomach and spleen, harmonizes the intestine, forces Qi, reduces moisture, nourishes blood and Yi, harmonizes lungs Qi, strengthens Qi and kidney Jing, moisturizes, relaxes, builds up Qi, spreads.
Cooking time approx. 10 min
Calories p. portion: 210
2 portions
Allergens: GO

**Quantity of ingredients**
Basic recipe for a rice soup (Congee)  4 cups / 500g. ......................*
Butter organic  1/2 teaspoon / 5g. .............................................. earth
Apricot dried  6 table spoons / 50g. ......................................... earth
Water  1/2 cup / 50g. (yes) ...................................................... earth
Maple syrup  1 dash / 3g. ...................................................... earth

**Cooking instructions:**
Cook rice congee according to basic recipe.

Melt a small amount of butter over a low heat and briefly fry small dried fruit with 1/2 cup of water. Add the amount
of rice porridge desired for the meal and heat. Serve hot and sweeten with maple syrup if necessary.
Variant: In addition fresh fruit with braise.

## 9.47 Rice dulse soup

Strengthens spleen and liver, regulates Qi flow, relaxes, builds up Qi, spreads, dries out, passes downwardly, strengthens stomach Qi, warms the stomach and spleen, harmonizes the intestine, forces Qi, reduces moisture.
Cooking time approx. 5 min
Calories p. portion: 190
2 portions
Allergens: L

**Quantity of ingredients**
Basic recipe for a rice soup (Congee)  4 cups /  500g. ......................*
Basic recipe for a vegetable soup (nutritious)  2 cup /  500g.  ............*
Dulse (seaweed)  2 table spoons /  15g. ....................................water

**Cooking instructions:**
Worm up a portion of pre-cooked basic recipe for a ricesoupe (congee) and a portion pre-cooked basic recipe for a vegetable soup.
Bake the dulse in the oven at 220 degrees for 3 minutes. Spread the crisp dulse over the rice.

## 9.48 Rice noodle soup with shiitake mushrooms

Strengthens spleen and liver, regulates Qi flow, relaxes, builds up Qi, spreads, dries out, passes downwardly, strengthens stomach Qi, nourishes Yin of the lungs, stomach and colon, supports digestion, reduces internal wind.
Cooking time approx. 20 min
Calories p. portion: 66
2 portions
Allergens: L

**Quantity of ingredients**

Rice noodles  2 handful / 20g. ...................................................metal
Shiitake, dried  4-6 pieces / 5g. ............................................... earth
Basic recipe for a vegetable soup (nutritious)  1 1/2 cups / 240g. ......*
Chinese cabbage  1 cup / 60g. ................................................ earth
Lovage  1 teaspoon / 3g. ........................................................metal
Miso  2 table spoons / 18g. .....................................................water

**Cooking instructions:**

Soak rice noodles and shiitake mushrooms separately in cold water. Heat the vegetable broth and add the soaked shiitake mushrooms cut into strips and simmer gently. Cut Chinese cabbage into noodles, add lovage green and rice noodles and let it steep for a while. Before serving, stir in Miso dissolved in a little cooled water.

Recommendation: Suitable at the beginning of each meal, also for breakfast

## 9.49  Rice soup with grated carrots and fresh herbs

Strengthens spleen and liver, regulates Qi flow, moisturizes, relaxes, builds up Qi, spreads, forces kidney and bladder.
Cooking time approx. 5 min
Calories p. portion: 131
4 portions
Allergens: EG

**Quantity of ingredients**

Rice wild (nature rice)  1 cup / 100g. .........................................metal
Water  6 cups / 700g. (yes) ...................................................... earth
Carrot  1 piece / 100g. ............................................................. earth
Soy sauce  1 dash / 2g. ...........................................................water
Butter organic  1 teaspoon / 3g. ............................................... earth
Ground  1 pinch / 0,3g. ............................................................ earth
Curcuma  1 pinch / 0,2g. .................................................................*
Herbs various  1 teaspoon (chopped) / 3g. .......................................*

**Cooking instructions:**

In a portion of rice congee according to basic recipe, softly cook a grated carrot, add butter and soy sauce. Sprinkle with fresh herbs.
Spices and herbs: black cumin, turmeric, cardamom, parsley, sage, thyme, basil, rosemary.
Winter: parsnip, celery, onion, leek, pumpkin
Summer: tomatoes, zucchini, spring onion, radishes, arugula.

## 9.50 Roasted oatmeal with grapes compote

Moisturizes, relaxes, builds up Qi, spreads, forces Qi, warms the stomach and spleen, promotes blood circulation and conduction flow.
Cooking time approx. 25 min
Calories p. portion: 328
2 portions
Allergens: AO

**Quantity of ingredients**
Oat flakes roasted  1 cup /  120g. ...............................................metal
Grapes red  1 1/2 cups /  240g. ............................................... earth
Ginger fresh  1/2 teaspoon /  1g. ..............................................metal
Raisins  2 table spoons /  20g. .................................................. earth
Cinnamon ground  1 pinch /  1g. ......................................................*
Water  1 1/2 cups /  200g. (yes)................................................ earth

**Cooking instructions:**
Roast the oats briefly, pour over water, add raisins and cook while, stirring for 20 min. Add grapes, ginger and cinnamon.

## 9.51 Sliced lamb with rosemary potatoes

Strengthens spleen and kidney Yang and stomach Qi, relieves weakness, heats middle and lower heater, forces
 Qi, relieves inflammation, moisturizes, relaxes, builds up Qi, spreads.
Cooking time approx. 1 hour
Calories p. portion: 461
4 portions
Allergens: LO

**Quantity of ingredients**
Lamb meat  7/8 lbs - 1 lbs /  500g. ................................................ fire
Olive oil  2 table spoons /  20g. ................................................. earth
Onion white  1 piece /  50g. .....................................................metal
Garlic  1 clove /  2g. ................................................................metal
Nutmeg  1 pinch /  0,2g. ..........................................................metal
Carrot  3 pieces /  150g. .......................................................... earth
Celery root  1/4 tuber /  120g. .................................................. earth
Rosemary  1 Twig /  3g. ............................................................. fire
Savory  1 teaspoon /  2g. .........................................................water
Parsley  1 table spoon /  8g. .................................................... wood
Pepper powder (hot)  1 pinch /  2g. ............................................ fire
Red wine  1/2 cup /  125g. ......................................................... fire

Salt (herbal)  1 pinch /  1g. ................................................water
Lemon juice  1/2 piece /  15g. ................................................wood
Cranberry  1 table spoon /  10g. ................................................wood
Potato  6 pieces /  400g. ................................................ earth

**Cooking instructions:**
Cut the lamb into strips, cut the carrots and celery into small cubes.
  Heat the olive oil in a pan, fry the lamb in it, add the cut onions and
garlic, salt with herbal salt, a little water, parsley, deglaze with red wine,
season with paprika and small cut rosemary, mugwort, savory, carrots
and celery, turn the heat back on small Simmer for about 35 minutes.
Season with pepper and nutmeg, if necessary still salt, add a little lemon
juice, season with paprika, cranberries.

Cut the potatoes in half, the length of, spread a little olive oil on the cut
surface, salt, sprinkle 2-3 rosemary needles
 on each half potato, place the potatoes on the baking sheet and bake in
a preheated oven for approx. 25 minutes at 190°C/374°F.

# 9.52 Spelled-grid porridge with berries of the season

Nourishes fluids, moisturizes dryness, produces humors, moisturizes
intestines, cools inner heat, preserves the fluids, contracts, forces middle,
nourishes heart and liver-blood, preserves the fluids, contracts.
Cooking time approx. 15 min
Calories p. portion: 244
2 portions
Allergens: AGH

**Quantity of ingredients**
Cow's milk (1.5% fat)  1/2 cup /  125g. ................................................*
Water  1/2 cup /  125g. (yes) ................................................ earth
Spelled semolina  5 table spoons /  50g. ................................................wood
Butter organic  2 teaspoons /  20g. ................................................ earth
Berries of the season  1/4 lbs - 4oz /  100g. ................................................wood
Honey  1-2 teaspoons /  5g. ................................................ earth
Almond  1-2 teaspoons /  5g. ................................................ earth
Peppermint  3-4 leaves /  2g. ................................................metal
Cinnamon ground  1 pinch /  0,5g. ................................................*
Vanilla  1 pinch /  0,2g. ................................................*
Cocoa  1 pinch /  0,5g. ................................................ fire
Coconut grated  1 table spoon /  10g. ................................................ earth

**Cooking instructions:**
Stir in spelled semolina in cold water and boil slowly over medium heat. After boiling, remove from the heat and let
simmer for a few minutes. Depending on the desired consistency, some water may have to be added. Stir in the butter and fine grated nuts in the mash and raspberries. Serve with honey or whole-grain sugar as desired. Spices and aromas: fresh mint, cinnamon or vanilla, cocoa, coconut

Summer: raspberries, blueberries, strawberries

## 9.53 Sweet polenta with peach

Nourishing and warming, harmonizes the middle.
Cooking time approx. 20 min
Calories p. portion: 330
2 portions
Allergens: GHO

**Quantity of ingredients**
Water  1 1/2 cups /  240g. (yes)................................................. earth
Corn Grease (Polenta)  1 cup /  100g. ......................................... earth
Butter organic  1/2 teaspoon /  2g. .............................................. earth
Barley malt  1/2 teaspoon /  2g. ................................................. earth
Cinnamon ground  1 pinch /  0,2g. ......................................................*
Cardamom  1 pinch /  0,2g. .............................................................*
Salt  1 pinch /  0,5g. ...........................................................water
Lemon  1 dash /  1g. ...........................................................wood
Raisins  2 table spoons /  20g. .................................................. earth
Apple juice (natural cloudy)  until covered /  10g. ........................ earth
Peaches  2 pieces /  240g. ....................................................... earth
Hazelnuts  2 table spoons /  20g. ............................................... earth

**Cooking instructions:**
Heat water till it boils. Stir in the polenta with a whisk and until tender; add some butter or cream, barley malt or maple syrup, cinnamon, some cardamom, a pinch of salt, a few drops of lemon juice and stir well.

Separately prepare a compote:
In a hot pot, simmer raisins in some apple or apricot juice for a few minutes; add fully ripe peaches chopped and heat; pour over the polenta served on plates; sprinkle with roasted nuts as desired.

## 9.54 Sweet rice with apples

Warming and nourishing, forces the middle.
Cooking time approx. 25 min
Calories p. portion: 156
4 portions
Allergens: H

**Quantity of ingredients**
Rice sweet  1 cup / 100g. ......................................................metal
Water  6 cups / 600g. (yes) .................................................... earth
Apple juice (natural cloudy)  1 cup / 120g. ............................... earth
Apple (sweet)  2 pieces / 300g. ............................................... earth
Apricot  2 pieces / 200g. ........................................................ earth
Cinnamon ground  1 pinch / 0,3g. ................................................... *
Cardamom  1 pinch / 0,2g. ............................................................. *
Ginger powder  1 knife tip / 0,3g. ...........................................metal
Salt  1 pinch / 0,3g. ................................................................water
Lemon  1/2 cut into pieces / 10g. .............................................wood
Cocoa  1 pinch / 0,5g. ............................................................ fire
Almond puree  2 table spoons / 20g. ....................................... earth
Barley malt  1 table spoon / 10g. ............................................. earth
Hazelnuts  2 table spoons / 20g. ............................................. earth

**Cooking instructions:**
Cook sweet rice in hot water.
Then: heat apple juice in a hot pot; chopped sweet apples, apricots or
other sweet fruit (neutral or warm), cinnamon, cardamom, ginger, a pinch
of salt, grated lemon peel, a little cocoa and simmer for a few minutes.

Stir in the boiled sweet rice, a little almond paste, some barley malt and
heat; sprinkle with roasted nuts.

## 9.55 Tea from ginseng

Forces heart, lungs, stomach, spleen, kidney-Qi.
Cooking time approx. 20 min
Calories p. portion: 0
4 portions

**Quantity of ingredients**
Ginseng  2 teabags /  4g. .................................................................\*
Water  2 cup /  500g. (yes).................................................... earth

**Cooking instructions:**
A very mild form of taking ginseng is achieved by placing it in a thermos of hot water. You can also use the root several times, not just for a pot filling. Ideally, you should have cooked the water for 10 minutes - it is then assigned to the conversion phase of fire - and to use non-carbonated medicinal spring water, if the quality of the water on site is not good.

Ingestion: This mild ginseng tea can be drunk throughout the day for strengthening.

# 9.56 Warming porridge

Forces Qi and defensive power.
Cooking time approx. 10 min
Calories p. portion: 357
1 portions
Allergens: AHO

**Quantity of ingredients**
Oat flakes (whole grain)  6 table spoons /  60g. .........................metal
Fig dried  3 pieces /  15g. ........................................................ earth
Star anise  1 piece /  1g. ...............................................................\*
Ginger fresh  1 pinch /  0,5g. ...................................................metal
Water  1 cup /  120g. (yes)....................................................... earth
Maple syrup  1 table spoon /  10g. ........................................... earth
Walnuts  1 table spoon (chopped) /  8g. ................................... earth

**Cooking instructions:**
Soak the dried fruit. Roast Oatmeal dry. Add dried ginger, star anise or cinnamon, a little grated ginger and boil everything with water to a mash. With maple syrup sweet. Whip grated walnuts and sprinkle before serving.

Effect: Suitable for the cold season.
Caution: Fresh ginger does not drink over a long period of time.

# 10 Herbs and their effects

## 10.1 Basil

thermal effect: warm
taste:spicy, bitter
Dries out, leads down. Tonifies Yang and Qi, dissolves mucus-cold, eliminates wind-cold.
It has a beneficial effect on flatulence and nausea, relaxing and soothing. Good to fight emphysema, bronchitis, whooping cough, high blood pressure, headache, mouth odor, warts, hiccup, gout, migraine.

## 10.2 Mugwort

thermal effect: warm
taste:bitter, spicy
Regulates and nourishes bleeding, warms the inside, eliminates wind-cold, eliminates parasites, eliminates heat, wetness, regulates and moves Qi.
Reduces bleeding, alleviates pain. In the kitchen, mugwort is used as a spice for fat food. Since it contains many bitter substances, it boosts fat burning and promotes digestion.

## 10.3 Savory

thermal effect: warm
taste:bitter
Tonifies kidney yang, heart qi, stomach and spleen qi and warms the middle, moves the liver qi and blood, releases mucous and cold from the lungs, opens the surface, induces wind-cold.
Stomach-strengthening, soothing and appetizing. Ideal for prevent colds, strengthens the immune system. In case of incontinence or nocturnal wetting (not for children), put the beans in liquor for libido.

## 10.4 Coriander

thermal effect: warm
taste:spicy
Driving sweat, reducing wind, draining moisture, tonifying and regulating qi, eliminating wind-cold.
The essential oils are appetizing, digestive, cramping and soothing in stomach and intestinal disorders.

## 10.5 Herbs various

Stimulates appetite. Effect different.
Appetizing, lots of trace elements and vitamins.

## 10.6 Chives

thermal effect: warm
taste:spicy
Directs upward. Tonifies blood, kidney Yang and Qi. Dissolves moisture.
Bactericide, prevents cancer, strengthens gastric juice production,
promotes digestion and blood circulation, promotes growth, triggers
stagnation.

## 10.7 Lovage

thermal effect: warm
taste:spicy, bitter
Reduces inner wind and moisture, dissolves stagnation, directs upward,
warms Yang, regulates and moves Qi, warms inside, dissolves mucus-
cold, eliminates wind-cold.
Stimulates digestion, reduces pain. Extracts of the root are used to flush
out urinary tract infections and prevent kidney gravel.

## 10.8 Lily bulbs

thermal effect: cool
taste:sweet, bitter
Tonifies Yin, soothes Shen / Spirit. Moisturizes the lungs, clears heat and
stops coughing.
Calms nerves, good to fight  scaly skin. The onions and the petals are
added to ointments in the Orient, which can heal muscles and tendons.
White lily (astringent).

## 10.9 Oregano fresh

thermal effect: warm
taste:bitter
Dries out, directs down, regulates and moves Qi, eliminates wind-cold,
soothes Shen / Spirit, suppresses inner wind, warms inside, eliminates
wind-cold / heat-wetness, moves blood, dissolves slime-cold.
It has an anti-digestive, calming and nerve-strengthening effect, helps to
fight cramping stomach and intestinal disorders. The ingredient Carvacrol
has an anti-inflammatory effect.

## 10.10   Parsley

thermal effect: warm
taste:bitter
Nourishes blood and liver, harmonizes liver and spleen, strengthens eyesight, preserves juices, contracts. Dissolves moisture and warms Yang.
Stimulates liver function, detoxifies. Forces urinating. Relieves flatulence. Digestive and menstrual stimulating, birth-accelerating, memory-enhancing, blood-purifying, skin-smoothing.

## 10.11   Peppermint

thermal effect: cool
taste:spicy, bitter
Cools heat, expels mucus, dissipates wind-cold and wind-heat, moves stomach qi, releases congestion, tonifies, regulates and moves qi.
Relaxes, frees the lungs and the nose (inhale), regulates the cycle. Stimulates bile flow and bile production, antispasmodic in gastrointestinal disorders, antimicrobial and antiviral.

## 10.12   Rosemary

thermal effect: warm
taste:bitter
Dries out, leads down. Strengthens the heart, lungs and spleen qi, strengthens liver blood. Strengthens heart-Yin. Expels spleen heat / cold moisture. Strengthens spleen and kidney yang.
Promotes digestion, relieves bloating, strengthens lung, spleen and kidney. Affects the circulation and nerves. Appetizing. Baths help to fight circulatory disorders as well as with gout and rheumatism.

## 10.13   Sage

thermal effect: neutral
taste:bitter, spicy
Expels slime, guides down, strengthens Qi, eliminates Wind-Heat, eliminate heat induced by Yin deficiency.
Good to fight yeast infections. The leaves have a digestive effect and are used in greasy foods. Antiperspirant effect.
Helps to relieve coughing attacks. Dries out.

## 10.14   Black caraway

thermal effect: warm
taste:spicy, sweet
Dissolve / transform moisture, tonifyes Yang and Qi, moves blood,
suppresses inner wind.
Detoxifying, immunoregulatory. In addition, the oil should stimulate the
formation of bone marrow cells and generally protect body cells from
viruses.

## 10.15   King Solomon's-seal

thermal effect: neutral
taste:sweet, bitter
Tonifies Yin and Qi, astringent, tonifies blood, eliminates wind-cold / heat-
wetness.
Used to repair wounds or damaged tissue. Good to fight dry cough,
earlier also tuberculosis and dysentery, as well as diarrhea and
hemorrhoids.

## 10.16   Yam root, yam root tuber

thermal effect: neutral
taste:sweet
Tonifies Yin, Yang and Qi, reduces inner wind, dissolves wetness, warms
Yang.
Solves cramps (in the gastrointestinal tract). Digestive through increased
bile production. Anti-inflammatory in rheumatic diseases.
Mucolytic agent for coughing. Relief of menopausal symptoms.

## 10.17   Lemongrass

Diverting, calming.
Reduction of flatulence, antimicrobial, appetizing. Prevention of influenza.
Good to fight infections in the mouth and throat.
----

## 10.18   Lemon Balm (fresh)

thermal effect: cool
taste: sour
Soothes Shen / Spirit, regulates and moves Qi, eliminates heat caused
by Yin deficiency, tones Qi.
Stimulating, antibacterial, encouraging, relaxing, antispasmodic, cooling,

antipyretic, analgesic, sweat-inducing, virus-inhibiting. Good for colds, fever, flu, cough, bronchitis, asthma, loss of appetite, bloating, heartburn.

# 11 Basics of Nutrition

The basic principles of nutrition described herein are general recommendations. They are not aimed at a specific form of therapy. Recommendations concerning a therapy have priority.

## 11.1 Nutrition

Regular meals in a relaxed atmosphere. A warm breakfast is considered a good start into the day.
The main meals ought to be taken for lunch – supper in the early evening. Pay attention to feeling hungry or sated: don't eat too much nor remain hungry is the rule
Prepare the meals freshly from natural, regional products. Frozen, heat-conserved, industrially prepared or foodstuffs cooked in the microwave oven are rejected.
Choice of foodstuffs according to the season: more cooling food in summer, more warming food in winter.
Eat cooked food at least twice a day. Food and drinks ought to be lukewarm, never ice-cold or hot.
Raw vegetables, briefly cooked vegetables, freshly squeezed juices and mineral water are not recommended. Milk and dairy products are only included in the diet if they don't cause problems. Don't use therapeutic recipes over a longer period without consulting your doctor or therapist.

**Varied food**
Enjoy the diversity of foodstuffs. Characteristics of a balanced nutrition are variety, suitable combination and a balanced quantity of rich and low energy foodstuffs (on one hand avoiding undersupply with essential nutrients and on the other hand to take to many undesirable substances).

**A lot of Cereal Products - and Potatoes**
Bread, pasta, rice, cereal flakes (best wholemeal) as well as potatoes contain almost no fat, but many vitamins, mineral nutrients, trace elements, roughage and secondary plant substances. These foodstuffs ought to be taken with low-fat side dishes.

**Vegetables and Fruit – „Take Five" every day ...** 5 portions of vegetables and fruit a day, as fresh as possible, briefly cooked, or maybe one portion as a juice – ideal as a side dish to every meal as well as snack between meals: Thus a lot of vitamins, mineral nutrients as well as roughage and secondary plant substances

**Daily milk and dairy products**

Milk and Dairy Products every Day, once or twice per Week Fish; meat, sausages as well as eggs moderately. These foodstuffs contain valuable nutrients like calcium in the milk, iodine selenium and omega-3 fat acids in saltwater fish. Meat is favorable due to its high content of disposable iron and the vitamins B1, B6 and B12. Quantities of 300 – 600 g meat and sausage per week are sufficient. Prefer low-fat products, especially in meat- and dairy products.

**Low-fat and fatty Foodstuffs**
Fat supplies us with essential fat acids and fatty foodstuffs contain also fat-soluble vitamins. Fat is high in energy; therefore much fat in the food may cause overweight, possibly also cancer. Too many saturated fat acids may further a tendency for cardio-vascular diseases in the long term. Prefer vegetable oils and fats (e.g. rapeseed-, olive-, soya-oils and solid fats produced therefrom). Beware of invisible fat in meat- and dairy products, pastry and sweets as well as in fast-food and convenience foods. 70 – 90 g fat per day is sufficient.

**Moderately Sugar and Salt**
Take sugar and foods/drinks containing various kinds of sugar (e.g. glucose syrup) only occasionally. Use herbs and spices as well as a little salt creatively. Prefer salt containing iodine.

**Plenty of Liquids**
Water is absolutely essential. Drink 1-2 l liquids every day. Prefer water (with or without gas) and other low-calorie drinks. Alcoholic drinks should not be taken.

**Tasty Dishes, carefully cooked**
Cook the meals with as low temperatures and as short as possible, using little water and fat – this preserves the original taste, keeps the nutrients intact and prevents the production of harmful compounds.

**Take time and enjoy the food**
Take your Time and enjoy your Food
Eating consciously helps to eat right. The eye enjoys food, too. It's fun, invites to enjoy varied dishes and stimulates the feeling of satiety.

**Watch your Weight and stay in Motion**
A balanced diet and a lot of exercise and sport (30 – 60 min/day) are a healthy combination. The right weight furthers well-being and health.
Thermals, directional effectiveness, digestive power
There are various criteria for judging the effectiveness of herbs and

foodstuffs.

The use of certain herbs and ingredients is based on observations of the effects on the body which these foodstuffs, herbs and spices show after having eaten them. The medical science has developed following system: Every ingredient or herb has a directional effectiveness. Furthermore, there are herbs which have a special effect on certain organs.

The basic condition for a healthy metabolism is to obtain sufficient energy from food and that the digestive process doesn't use too much energy. An easily digestible meal makes content and sated, doesn't cause flatulence and fatigue after the meal. The perfect spices increase the healthiness of our meals. Very often, just small doses of herbs and spices will suffice. They are not used to make us sated, but to help our digestive organs to digest the food.


## 11.2 Recipes

The recipes list the ingredients to be used and the cooking instructions show how the dish is prepared. The list of ingredients shows the concerned quantities as well as the relevance for the therapy. If you find „less than mentioned", try to comply or find an alternative from the „list of recommended foodstuffs". Mostly it shall result just in a small change of taste when you simply avoid this ingredient.

Mild cooking methods: boiling, stewing, poaching, steaming
Strong cooking methods: barbecuing, roasting, frying, smoking
Balanced cooking methods: deep-frying, baking brick
Deep-freezing and warming in the microwave oven should be avoided (denaturalization).


## 11.3 Foodstuffs

Foodstuffs have an effect on body and soul like medicinal herbs, only a very much milder one. Dietary advice is mainly based on regional foodstuffs. The knowledge about the effects of each foodstuff and the knowledge, when which foodstuff shall be used, is based on the orthodox school of medicine. Use ecologic-organic products, if possible. As everything should be cooked for a long time due to a better digestability and very rarely eaten raw, the food agrees with everyone.

The classification of the foodstuffs according to their effect on the body is the basis in order to achieve a harmonious status of health.

Dietary advisors do not recommend certain foodstuffs for everyone. The individual diet is tailor-made for the individual constitution.

Buy only fresh and ripe fruit and vegetables. You ought to leave unripe fruit and vegetables and such with brown spots and wilted leaves behind in the market. In this case take deep-frozen goods (never ready-to-serve dishes!). Fruit and vegetables are deep-frozen immediately after harvesting and often contain more vitamins and minerals than the goods from the vegetable shelf. Whereas conserved or tinned goods contain very much less biological substances. Also, salt, sugar and others are mostly added to the latter. Never leave the foodstuffs in the water after washing them to avoid that many vital substances get drowned. Clean salads, fruit and vegetables immediately before serving.

Please make sure of the hygienic processing of foodstuffs. Clean your salads, fruit and vegetables carefully. When cooking with meat, prepare all ingredients first and then process the meat products. Clean the worktop and tools very carefully. Wooden surfaces ought to be treated with a mild disinfectant regularly in order to reduce germination. Store fruit and vegetables separately, if possible. Harvested fruit and vegetables are still alive and emit e.g. ethylene gas, which makes other products ripen and age faster. Keep meat and fish in the closed packaging or store them in the fridge in closed containers.

## 11.4 Herbs

There are some basic rules for storing medicinal herbs. On principle, herbs must be protected from direct sunlight, humidity and heat.

Containers for the storage of herbs may be glasses, ceramic jars and even plastic containers. However, plastic is a rather unsuitable material and should only be a short-term solution. In case of glass containers, use a dark material.

Medicinal herbs cannot be kept for any long period. The shelf life of herbs is limited. However, it can be prolonged with suitable storage. The place should be dark, rather cool and absolutely dry. A wooden medicine cabinet, placed not directly next to a source of heat, would be ideal. Never buy large quantities of herbs so as not to have to throw them away. Label the container with the name of the herb and the date of harvesting or processing.

# 12 Other dietic-books

The following syndromes of dietetics, TCM or for a therapy supplement for cancer are available.

## Dietetics

E001. Nutrition of the infant - baby food
E002. Nutrition during lactation
E003. Nutrition in old age
E004. Nutrition of children and adolescents
E005. Nutrition of athletes
E006. Light weight
E007. Pregnancy
E008. Full food

**Protein and electrolyte - kidneys**
E009. (hemodialysis) dialysis treatment
E010. Acute renal failure
E011. Chronic renal insufficiency
E012. Nephrotic syndrome
E013. Kidney stones (nephrolithiasis)

**Gastrointestinal tract - pancreas**
E014. Acute pancreatitis (inflammation of the pancreas)
E015. Chronic pancreatitis (inflammation of the pancreas)

**Gastrointestinal tract - small intestine and large intestine**
E016. Acute obstipation (constipation)
E017. Chronic obstipation (constipation)
E018. Colon irritabile
E019. Diverticulitis
E020. Acquired lactose intolerance (lactose malabsorption)
E021. Fructose malabsorption
E022. Glutensensitive enteropathy (celiac disease)
E023. Colectomy
E024. Short Bowel Syndrome

**Gastrointestinal tract - liver, gallbladder, bile ducts**
E025. Acute and chronic hepatitis (inflammation of the liver)
E026. Cholelithiasis (bile stones)
E027. fatty liver
E028. cirrhosis

**Gastrointestinal tract - Stomach and duodenal intestine**
E029. Acute gastritis
E030. Chronic gastritis
E031. Stomach bleeding
E032. Ulcus ventriculi and duodenal ulcer
E033. Condition after gastric surgery

**Gastrointestinal tract - oral cavity and esophagus**

E034. Stomatitis
E035. Esophageal carcinoma (esophageal cancer)
E036. Refluosophagitis (heartburn)

**Special diseases**
E037. Phenylketonuria (PKU)
E038. Rheumatic joint diseases

E039. **Metabolism** Obesity (overweight)
E040. Diabetes mellitus
E041. Eating disorders (underweight)

**Fat metabolism**
E042. Hypercholesterolaemia (increased cholesterol level)
E043. Hepatic Encephalopathy

**Heart and circulation**
E044. Arteriosclerosis (arterial calcification)
E045. Heart insufficiency
E046. Hypertension
E047. Hyperuricaemia and gout

E048. **Changed nutrient requirements** In case of fever
E049. For malignant diseases
E050. After burns
E051. Radiation and chemotherapy

E100. **CANCER** Pancreatic cancer
E101. Bladder cancer
E102. Blood cancer (leukemia)
E103. Breast cancer
E104. Colorectal cancer
E105. Gastric cancer
E106. Kidney cancer
E107. Esophageal cancer

E200. **TCM** Bladder - moisture heat in the bladder Bladder - moisture and cold in the bladder Bladder - emptiness and cold in the bladder
E201. Large intestine - external cold affects the large intestine Large intestine - moisture heat in the large intestine
E202. Large intestine - heat blocks the intestine II acute
E203. Large intestine - dryness of the colon
E204. Large intestine - Yang deficiency (cold)
E205. Heart - Blood insufficiency
E206. Heart - Blood stagnation
E207. Heart - Fire
E208. Heart - Hot mucus clogs the heart pores
E209. Heart - Cold mucus clogs the heart pores
E210. Heart - Qi deficiency
E211. Heart - Yang deficiency
E212. Heart - Yin deficiency
E213. Liver - Ascending Liver Yang
E214. Liver - Blood deficiency
E215. Liver - Blood stagnation

E216. Liver - Moisture heat in liver and gall bladder Liver - Fire
E217. Liver - Gall bladder Qi-Empty Liver - Cold in the liver meridian
E218. Liver - Qi stagnation Liver - Wind Liver - Wind with ascending liver Yang
E219. Liver - Wind with blood anemic
E220. Liver - Wind with extreme heat
E221. Lung - Qi deficiency Lung - Mucus-moisture in the lungs
E222. Lung - Mucus-heat in the lungs
E223. Lung - Mucus-cold in the lungs
E224. Lung - Dryness of the lungs
E225. Lung - Wind-heat attacks the lungs
E226. Lung - Wind-cold affects the lungs
E227. Lung - Yin deficiency
E228. Stomach - Bloodstagnation Stomach - Fire
E229. Stomach - Cold with liquid
E230. Stomach - Nutrition stagnation
E231. Stomach - Qi deficiency
E232. Stomach - Rebellious Qi
E233. Stomach - Yin Emptiness
E234. Spleen - Heat and moisture attack the spleen
E235. Spleen - Coldness and moisture affects the spleen
E236. Spleen - Qi deficiency
E237. Spleen - Qi deficiency + Declining spleen Qi
E238. Spleen - Qi deficiency + spleen does not control the blood
E239. Spleen - Yang deficiency
E240. Kidney - Heart and kidney no longer communicate
E241. Kidney - Jing deficiency
E242. Kidney - Kidneys cannot receive the Qi
E243. Kidney - Qi is not stable
E244. Kidney - Yang deficiency
E245. Kidney - Yin deficiency


For further information visit di-book.com.